The Cosmic Cradle

Lessons and Poetry
on Living Life with a Lifted Spirit

by
Beloved Heartsong

Revised Edition
© 2013 Beloved Heartsong

ISBN 978-0-974981-2-4 (sc)
ISBN 978-0-9749810-1-7 (pdf ebook)
Also available on Kindle

First Edition
© 2004 ISBN 0-9749810-0-1 (out of print)

All rights reserved, including the right of reproduction in whole or in part, in any form.

Visit Beloved on the Web:

Beloved's Music:
www.BelovedHeartsong.com

LaHo-Chi Institute of Energy Healing:
www.LaHoChi.org

Other Offerings:
www.OpenYourHearts.com

Email:
beloved@openyourhearts.com

Dedication

There are those who bend and shape you and those who tend to your growth with love and care. I am truly blessed to be able to say most of the people in my life, friends and family, have fit into both categories simultaneously. To All I am grateful, for the love I live now is the fruit of fertile ground.

To my parents, brother, and grandparents, the gift of your undying support and love in my life has created the most comprehensive and beautiful understanding of cradle.

To my children, who taught me how to cradle them and all of life in the fullest sense, thank you for being such magnificent teachers.

To my extended family and friends, thank you for your love and light — how blessed we are to dance together!

To God, the Beloved, reflected in all eyes and in all of life, all of who I am sings gratitude for infinite Union.

Contents

My Experience 7
Foreword 9

Completeness 14
Open 15

Conscious Presence 18
Time to Begin 19

Joining Heart and Higher Self 22
Loving Presence 23

Magic 26
We Wizards... 27

Coloring Perceptions 32
Color Your World 33

Flow 36
As the Current Takes You... 37

Merry-Go-Round 40
Today and Every Day 41

Pain 44
Go Into the Darkness... 45

Change 48

Renewed Vitality 52
Inner Light 53

Peace 56
Now More Than Ever 57

Love 60
Glory Be... 62

Grace **66**
   The Choice of One 68

Direction, Motivation, and Completion **72**
   Stand Tall 74
   Earth Mother 75

Everlasting Joy **78**
   Be Childlike 79
   Please, Please Me... 81

Thought Control and Emotion **86**
   Affirmation 87
   Set Yourself Free.. 88

Lift Your Spirit **92**
   The Window of Love 93

Patience **96**
   Learning to Live in the Moment 97
   In Gratitude 99

Breathing **102**
   As I Breathe 104

The Union of Hearts, Souls, and Minds
Is the Gift of Music **108**
   Overtones 109
   Music 111

Joining Together as One **114**
   Oh Beloved 116

Invite Tomorrow In **120**
   Enter Into the Silence 121
   The Way Home 122
   Live Fully 123

About the Author **125**

My Experience

In my early twenties, I began exploring spirituality through books and talking to others. In 1995, I took my first workshop on a beautiful form of spiritual hands-on healing called LaHo-Chi. It was a powerful weekend that profoundly changed my life in many ways! I had no idea at the time that years later I would become an instructor and eventually the Director of the same LaHo-Chi Institute! I now travel and teach throughout the United States. (See my websites below for more information.)

- The LaHo-Chi Institute of Energy Healing: www.LaHoChi.org
- My Music Site: www.BelovedHeartsong.com
- My Original Site: www.OpenYourHearts.com

This amazing work opened all my subtle senses at once, enabling me to see, hear, know, feel, and understand very expanded levels of consciousness.

Soon after, I began receiving the poetry and messages in this book in their entirety. I never had to think or focus or revise; it just flowed effortlessly. I would hear the words in my head while I was in the shower, or while driving, or in my sleep and would feel compelled to wake up and write them down. At times, I felt bombarded with information, but I learned to listen with gratitude very quickly. The feeling of being embraced and cradled in great love was always present as I received each message or poem.

As I continued working with the LaHo-Chi energy, I

continued to joyfully embrace my spiritual growth, opening my heart and my consciousness more and more. It seemed the miracles and the flow of life were ever present and out-picturing in amazing ways. I began receiving and sharing specific messages and visions of love with and for others. As we benefited from this flow of Grace, I realized what a difference these beautiful gifts of Spirit were making in many lives — especially in my own life. The gifts continue to expand and flow, through my work with groups, individual clients, energetic healing, teaching, and music.

I feel so blessed and grateful to be rocked and held in this cradle of infinite love and to be able to share these simple, yet powerful lessons with others. As you read this book, I suggest that you use it to guide you to the pages that will offer you the IN-sights that will serve you best in each moment. As you receive the simple truths of each message or poem, allow your heart to open to yourself and to your joy. I invite you to open your mind to unlimited possibilities, allowing it to be shifted, lifted, and set free.

Namasté
Beloved Heartsong

Foreword

As infants and toddlers, most of us are blessed with parents who rock us, nurture and love us, make us feel safe, and help us heal.

As we mature and age, it becomes our responsibility to do this for ourselves. This unspoken transfer of power often leaves us feeling lonely, unsafe, unloved, unprotected, and frustrated, angry, and vulnerable. We feel like the baby in the lullaby: "When the bough breaks, the cradle will fall, and down will come baby, cradle and all."

The intention of these writings is to help us find the strength and courage to crawl back into the cosmic cradle that surrounds us all — Spirit. As we see ourselves and our world community interconnected by this common unity, this cosmic cradle, we can make it our own and love ourselves enough to open our hearts, to heal our wounds, and to honor and see the beauty within each and every One.

Loving and healing the cosmos is a journey that begins within the infinite nest of our own hearts — the Heart of One.

Written here, on these pages, is a journal of the journey of Spirit, yours and mine, as we remember who we really are — One with each other, God, our Source, the universal Love.

Allow yourself the time and space to turn inward and expand who you are into the cosmic cradle — the place where you are held, loved, and nurtured — where all your needs and desires are met.

This is the place of unity — where we have come from, and where we are going — Home.

Go forth my child, in strength and with courage. You are a child of the universe. You have the power to endure all that comes your way — with Grace and dignity and constant guidance. You are never alone. You are encircled and held in divine love.

Be at peace.

The Cosmic Cradle

COMPLETENESS

Completeness

Imagine the gift of Spirit without any manifestation on the physical realm, a great sense of completeness in knowing yourself fully as Spirit that is. This is not limited to the etheric realm.

Achieving and feeling a true sense of completeness within your soul is a gift of Self. It is an understanding, a knowing, and a profound peace that comes with the ever widening and deepening of the "Aha! We are One!"

The paradox of feeling complete here on Earth is in recognizing you need not know or gain or gather anything to be whole and complete — that with no-thing, you are and always have been All. The distinctions you have made all your life as to levels of divinity fall away and judgment is no longer necessary. You replace the painful process of separation with the joy, peace, and unity of Spirit. And once again you remember:

I am whole.
I am One.
I am complete.
I am God.

Open

Open unto the world a new dawn.
Open unto the world an unknown Grace.
Embrace the divinity among the heavens
that lies at the core of all beings.
Choose lightly to step upon another's path,
dancing through veils that mask the One.
Open to the unending love that is yours.
Choose it, so that in owning it, you may freely share it.
You are children of the light, keepers of the flame.
You have known yourselves as love in its purest form.
The divine spark of creation is the fire in your bellies.
Wear it proudly.
Allow it to consume and impassion
and empower all you are and all you do.
Live your life with the passion in your belly
and the love of the One in your heart.
Merge and unite all the parts of yourself.
Become One.

CONSCIOUS PRESENCE

Conscious Presence

Each moment is precious and is defined by how you use it. Consciously choosing your way shapes the direction and course that ultimately leads you Home. Going within is the path that helps you choose most wisely. Look to yourself for answers. Look to yourself for questions. Look to yourself for knowing.

Release all fears; they encircle you like a prison. Embrace what is yours by divine right...choose love in every moment.

Time to Begin

Be light-hearted in your endeavors.
Be free in your mind and your space.
Envision the rapture you desire.
Open to its unending grace.

Extend your bounds, take great pleasure,
in all that you say and you do.
Allow for the genie within you
to open your heart to the Truth.

Avoid holding fear as your friend.
Escape from the walls which confine.
Go in to that place deep inside you;
the Union of heart, soul, and mind.

Find in that place, the longing for Home
has found its true and infinite nest.
Open your heart to the center of One.
Feel its magnificence swell in your chest.

Envelop your being in its loving embrace.
Stand with your face to the wind.
The glory of God will power your soul.
Take a breath; it is time to begin.

JOINING HEART AND HIGHER SELF

Joining Heart and Higher Self

You are loved dearly.

Love is a gift that opens you to new and higher ground. Growing with it and within, you develop a higher sense of who you are and what you're about. As you stay directed, your path will unfold in the proper sequencing.

Joining your heart and your higher self — your inner wisdom — will give you the clarity you seek.

Loving Presence

Bring your loving presence here to me now.

Go into your heart,
it's from here you'll know how...
to seek your own glory,
to climb to the top,
The passage of time will just seem to stop.

The undying love of the cosmos is yours.
The passion of your own heart leads the grand tour...
through playgrounds of angels,
museums divine, oceans of bliss,
and in returning you'll find
that through all of your travels, wherever you roamed,
though distance perceived, you never left Home.

The uncorking of consciousness
through your own inner guide,
is the chariot with wings
you've been waiting to ride.
As your heart whispers to you,
to your own truth bow.

Bring your loving presence here to me now.

MAGIC

Magic

Magic comes when you least expect it. The magic you have at your fingertips is of beauty and magnificence. In every moment, you have the opportunity to follow your joy, your heart, your inspiration, and inner-guidance into the synchronicity and flow of what most people would call miracles. The alchemy of creation and Spirit moving into physical form is constantly directed and re-directed by your choices, focus, and thoughts.

Divine inspiration can come as thoughts, dreams, signs, feelings, visions, sounds, or knowing. Trusting in what you receive and how it feels to you, and choosing to honor it, allows this flow of Grace to continue to bless you and keeps your wand brimming with powerful magic.

You are forever blessed with the inclination to be magical. This power isn't really magic at all — it is yours by divine right, your spiritual connection, and all who walk this plane are blessed in the same way.

As you spiritually mature and evolve, you develop an appreciation and understanding of knowledge you previously found mysterious. It will unfold and seem magical. This "hocus-pocus" will take you to other dimensions. What was once believed to be magic outside of yourself becomes an inner knowing that is far more magical.

Your reality at any given moment is yours to bend and shape at will. Choose wisely. Wave your wand purposefully. You are blessed with magic!

We Wizards...

Magic seeps out through the cracks of our minds,
and oozes through doorways in the shadows of time.

It creaks up the stairways to the attic of our souls,
opening deep boxes with stories untold.

It shouts through our being to make us become
an expanded version of self through the One.

The alchemy stirs up the pot, and the brew
is the field we all play in — primordial stew.

Color and sound invite threads of divine...
consciousness transcending space and all time.

Magic that conjures up fairies and sprites,
visions and pleasures and basic delights.

Magic that challenges the old and the new...
magic that proves what has always been true:

> That we are unlimited;
> we shape our truths.

> That freedom we yearn for
> is, in fact, the real proof...

That magic lies deep within hearts, souls, and minds,
that we are bewitched by our own cords and lines.

That we can choose magic and break all the spells
that dropped us from heaven and created our hell.

That we are so powerful, so graceful, so fine,
we beings of light and love are divine!

Wizards we are, with wands filled with intention.
We carelessly wave them, we don't pay attention...
then remorsefully ask for divine intervention.

Envision the magic you wish to create.
What will you choose as your ultimate fate?

The magic you were born with has been yours all along.
Reach into your hat now...
the show must go on!

COLORING PERCEPTIONS

Coloring Perceptions

The quality or shape of light in any given moment is determined by your judgment alone. You "color" each perception yourself. You bend it and mold it until it takes the shape you feel comfortable with.

The good, the bad, and the ugly of it (the light, your experience) are all perceptions of the ego. Although we may perceive life as made up of dualities (light and dark, up and down, etc.), they are all aspects of One...One light, One love, One universe — that of God.

Color Your World

Choose to resemble the child within in your every endeavor.
Choose to break free of that which confines the Spirit.
Allow for the beauty and Grace of each moment
to unfurl and unfold all your hidden treasures.
See Spirit at work in all you do.
Paint the colors of your palette across the sky.
Be aware of the universal flow around you.
Seek to satisfy your inner knowings.
Be the peace you seek!
Send your love to the corners of the Earth —
and home again.
Lift your Spirit, time and time again.
Shift your perception.
See through the veils...
Love the One in You!!

FLOW

Flow

You can't continue to "reason out" all you do and feel. Flowing in the cosmic universe of love is all you need at any given time in your life.

When you swim upstream, every cell has to fight against the current, focusing on tasks it otherwise would not.

Let all of your BE-ing do what it naturally knows to do – flow, flow, flow....

Be gentle. Slow down. You **can** slow down. Ask yourself what is necessary. And...what is necessary will always make itself apparent. Allow the rest to fall aside and let gentleness take its place.

Be open to change in every way. Your life will take on new direction and meaning. Allow it to flow through, around, and within you. People in your life will bring purpose and meaning to the joys that abound. Live in the moment. Go with the flow. Stay centered in your truth. Let love and light shine forth from you and penetrate all of what you do and all of who you are. Let your heart spill forth – it is time for the joy within to be set free!

As the Current Takes You...

As the current takes you, let it flow.
As it wants to leave you, let it go.
Blossom as a flower; hold your face to the sun.
Love is where we're going and where we've come from.
As the current takes you, it's love you become.

** Note: This is a song from my CD "Forever Love."
To listen to excerpts of it, visit: BelovedHeartsong.com

MERRY-GO-ROUND

Merry-Go-Round

Around and around you spin on the merry-go-round of life. Where you sit and how fast you go are choices you make. Do you take it all in or are you going too fast to enjoy the ride? Ask yourself, "Am I having fun? Am I enjoying the view? What is it I see that I wish to explore further? What is it I see that no longer serves me and I wish to pass by? Who do I wish to take on my ride? Who shall I leave behind? Does my pace allow intimate connections with self? With others? With nature? With the divine? Do I feel out of control? Do I want to get off?"

Many times we let ourselves get to the point of jumping off before we notice we had the choice to slow down all along. If you choose a nurturing pace, dreams and visions will reflect the peace and calm you seek. Intimacies will occur frequently in all areas of your life. Joy and your heart's desires can manifest more fully because you can see more clearly and intend with less distraction.

"Stop the world! I want to get off!" does not need to be your mantra! Embracing gentleness, loving yourself enough to notice the parts of you that cry out for your attention, and choosing to nurture the changes that will enable and empower you will make the ride worthwhile. You will find that each seat on the merry-go-round is a new way to love yourself – a fresh perspective, an opening door. You'll begin to see and feel love was always around you in all that you viewed. You were just going too fast to notice before. Each day, as the music starts and your day begins, take a deep breath and *enjoy* the ride.

Today and Every Day

Today and every day, you are loved.

Today and every day, you are born anew.

Today and every day, you must do what you need to do
to ensure that all your dreams and goals stay in focus.

Today and every day, walk your path in love and light.

Today and every day, bless each moment,
for it is rich with wonder and unlimited possibilities.

Today and every day, you are One with the universe.

Today and every day, give thanks for being.

Today and every day, grow more wide-eyed and enthusiastic.

Today and every day, be at peace.

Today and every day, go within for answers.

Today and every day, judge not.

Today and every day, live in Grace.

Today is every day,
all your moments have brought you here.

Today is every day, it is all there is.

Today is every day...
live in the moment, here...now...forever...and for all time.

Today.

PAIN

Pain

Are you learning? Do you hear? Do you see? Do you smell? Taste? Feel? Know? Do you understand what your body wants you to know?

Your Higher Self encourages you to be here, now, in present time, at all times, in all senses. The reason you are made to or told to slow down is so it will be possible to experience life as expansively as possible. You have to slow down to "stop and smell the roses."

As your light expands, so does your opportunity to cast light on and explore your shadow. Surrender to it and go **through** it — you won't stay there...you'll move to "higher ground." Your pain is a teacher. As a student, trust in your guidance — the power of Spirit is bringing all to pass...

Go Into the Darkness...

Go into the darkness and seek yet your peace.
Go into the tunnels and bury your grief.

Choose to recover what you left there instead.
Dig up your possessions, fear not where you tread.

Remember and find all the gifts that you are.
Honor yourself, as you are a bright star.

Reclaim your heart's truth,
feel the flame in your breast.

Grasp onto your power
as it swells in your chest.

See your Grace and beauty in everyone's eyes.
Know this reflection is really your prize.

Acknowledge the wisdom that comes from within.
Own who you are, this is where you begin.

Find your buried treasure and bring it to light;
sift through it with passion and joy and delight!

Know more completely that you are divine.
Discovering yourself is just a matter of time.

As you learn to be gentle with the One in the mirror,
the reflection of love will become even clearer.

The gifts of our souls are the magnificence we share.
Go into the darkness and find yourself there.

CHANGE

Change

Change is what brings you hope. Change brings you desire and fulfills that longing for more, for new, for different, and for better.

Don't expect all your dreams in an afternoon. The pieces of the puzzle fall in place one by one. Your speed is determined by growth, attitude, loving openness, and receptivity to change.

Organizing your dreams won't help. Opening to new and higher ideas of uncertainty will.

"I feel a change coming on..."

RENEWED VITALITY

Renewed Vitality

Like magic, there are times when you awaken to a renewed and refreshed vitality. This is a further awakening and expansion of your core being. Light is the flow that allows for the "magical" enhancement of who you already are.

Visualizing a light within will bring clarity to focus upon your daily endeavors. Call upon that which is needed in the moment.

Growth comes in stages as you build light upon light, vision upon vision, knowing upon knowing. Allow for your Higher Presence to spill forth.

Going the distance is a matter of going with-IN. You are unlimited...

Inner Light

Of all the love in all the world,
none has burned so bright,
as the love discovered deep inside,
our own strong inner light.

We challenge ourselves with renewed hope,
in every passing day,
to become the One – in infinite scope,
and love along the way...

...to love in gladness, in joy, in peace,
to dwell in our own hearts in truth,
to open completely, with passion and freely
embrace what we came here to do.

...to be so magnificent,
that we sing the songs of angels here on Earth.
And we will know that we belong,
to that place in us that we know so well,
the infinite heart of the One...
where we dwell.

PEACE

Peace

Peace is a choice that many people fail to explore. So many feel it is elusive and something to wish or hope for – but it is simply a choice.

Whether you are choosing not to fight or choosing to exist in a gentle state of mind, peace is an option. If you look at peace clearly, you will find it is always available as yet another choice on your path.

In every moment you choose to be. What is it you are choosing to BE?

Be peace...
Be love...
Be joy...

Be...

Now More Than Ever...

Let yourself unfold.

Be the divine spark you are.

Allow grace to fill your world.

Allow love to light your path.

Honor your Mother.

Become One with your fears.

Illuminate your shadow.

Prove yourself worthy of your own love.

Extend your bounds.

Embrace your divinity.

Flow in your own cool waters.

Allow, expand, unfold, unite.

Now more than ever...

LOVE

Love

Love is a two-part process. First comes the enveloping of self in love, then what follows is always an outer manifestation of the first.

Love can only be for others when you have given it to the self. As you grow into a maturity of the love of self, you will notice the partners who come into your life will be more mature and evolved also.

Pain in love comes from holding yourself back from a fuller expression of self-love. If you cling to one who isn't ready or willing to mutually reflect the self's movement toward evolution, you limit what you can see and do for yourself — hence the pain. Instead, allow a new, more mature love into your life.

Joy comes from allowing yourself to expand love of self. Those who come into your life will be drawn through your mirror and will reflect back to you where you are in any given moment.

If you don't like what you see in front of you, go within to make changes, and allow those around you their own path. Holding on to people in your life who need to move on is just as difficult as trying to reach through a physical mirror to hold on to your reflection there. It is all illusion — the only thing that is real is the love in your own heart.

Grasping outside yourself for love always brings an empty hand — because you can't reach through a mirror.

Allowing your heart to fill with divine love — radiating inward to the self first — will bring the desired results. All those who come to you have come in response to what you are radiating. Notice and become conscious of what you bring to yourself. Be your own observer. Free the illusions from your idea of self and watch your love grow.

Love yourself as you wish to be loved.
No judgments, no grief — only love.

Glory Be...

Glory to God as the heavens shine down
upon all the children, their halos; their crowns.

Glory to be our infinite best,
judging no one and simply releasing the tests.

Glory on high as the wind sweeps our fears,
dissolving our anger, drying our tears.

Song of the angels rejoice in rebirth,
as we honor our Mother and nurture the Earth.

Holy reunion of hearts, souls, and minds,
holy communion for All through all time.

Joy intermingled with vanishing fears,
breaks through separation and brings the All here.
Glory in love that brings all to the Source...
a journey we all take; our most precious course.

Glory that shines through our eyes filled with love,
glory in peace on the wings of the dove.

Glory to God — for it's how we began.
Glory to the One who put wings on a man.

GRACE

Grace

How do you suppose life brought you to this point? Grace and love and wisdom are yours by divine right. But, think for a moment about how your will plays into every fork in the path as your entire life unfolds.

Cosmic Grace flows and is received effortlessly when beings are truly BEING. All kingdoms accept and flow and are part of this Grace. Only humans have the choice to block or alter their perception of the experience of this flow. It cannot be diminished — but the choice can be made to experience being "out of sync."

Know clearly, dear ones, that any place you feel discomfort in your lives, you have made an agreement or choice to believe in order to manifest the experience.

To return to the synchronicity of BEING — fully Being — you must choose to BE in the moment...fully present. This is where your joy is. This is where creation is. This is your only truth. This is where change is made and love is made manifest.

Cosmic Grace is complete support in unconditional love from God and the universe and the All that is. You are always of and filled with this Grace.

What you experience is always a result of (1) your choices, thoughts, and beliefs and (2) this complete support of your choices, thoughts, and beliefs.

Your idea or your belief that you are not blessed or graced because you are in pain is not truth, but you may take this belief as far as you wish — to create your own personal hell — if necessary — or, you may choose to go as high as you dare to dream — ascending here on Earth — merging and uniting all the parts of you with joy and love, gentleness and Grace — owning the God you are.

Remember, the Grace that blesses your existence is there for all to choose. For many, it does not seem to be an easy place to reach. Living in the flow enables not only yourself but others around you to see how it works, to feel its beauty, its "Grace" if you will. So, dear One...your joy, your light, your soul, your essence, your desire, and your choice is of your design, yet, it is not yours alone — it belongs to All that is and ever will be.

Shine forth.

The Choice of One

Today we have a choice:

to become the light beings we are,
to shine forth in God's gracious glory,
to forgive each trespass against us,
to fully enjoy and embrace each waking moment,
to teach every child of their inner beauty, wisdom,
and grace,
to touch the hearts and souls of all we meet
with the light of our love,
to send joy and rapture forth from our core,
to fill the world with enticing strands of love and devotion
for an undivided and unified heart,
a heart that will expand as a mighty ocean,
whose waves pound and wash away self-doubt and hatred,
surging again and again until the waters are illumined
with the power of the One.

One heart,
One mind,
One light,
One joy,
One passion,
One beloved,
One belief,
One moment,
One now,
One pulse;
The Infinite One.

DIRECTION, MOTIVATION, AND COMPLETION

Direction, Motivation, and Completion

The purpose of guidance is to assist you in making choices that allow for direction and purpose to fill your thoughts, enabling you to walk through life with confidence. This is guidance from your Higher Self and the angelics. In each moment you have the opportunity to access and use guidance that has been sifted down through your Higher Self. Acting on faith and following your own path strengthens the flow of clear communication and keeps the channel of guidance and direction open. Doubts and fears "muddy the waters" and bring in confusion.

To regain a clear line of communication, one must go into one's heart for answers. When you go into your heart, you will always have access to your Higher Self, purpose, and a clear channel of communication with your soul.

Your mind carries the agenda of the ego and attempts to sift through all the stimulation around you. This process isn't always easy to bypass — as many observe when first learning to meditate. As you explore your own questions and desires through your heart, the clarity and peace you seek will always be right there waiting for you.

Choosing your path becomes easier once you become clearer about what truly motivates you. Discerning between true motivation, your heart's desire, impulse, or habit is a key step. Have you ever wondered after the fact why you had done something? Choosing to embrace what truly motivates your heart brings you to a place beyond wondering...to a place of knowing.

Loving yourself through this process is important. Your heart will lead you if you let it. Doubts, fears, and regrets only reside in your mind. Listening to and following your heart will always illuminate the path of clear and loving direction – your motivation is the lightness of being you experience in this process. If you feel any doubt when exploring your heart, realize that it is only fear of choosing your true direction that inhibits you. Once again, a leap of faith is called for. It is the bridge to your heart, your soul's purpose, your true path and the way Home.

Completion of any task brings many mixed results – depending upon the clarity of intent and motivation. If you choose to look with and into your own heart, you will know who you are. Are you someone who honors or ignores your heart as it speaks to you? Do you allow or dismiss the Divine in its most personal expressions? Do you know yourself as the magnificence of the One? Are you honest about what motivates you? Do you love yourself as you answer these questions? Completion should bring you back to where you started – to the place of clear direction.

What motivates you?

Stand Tall

Stand tall as we gather around you.
Stand proud and without fear as thunder claps your ears.
Feel the flames of the sacred fire dance in your veins.

Join with the Spirit of the woods
and all the animals on your path.
Partake of the pipe of peace.
Stand tall and face Father Sun.
Bow to the moon and honor the Mother within.
Feel the wind at your back
as it guides you in each direction.

Earth and sky, fire and water;
we are all this and more.
Listen in the stillness to your own Spirit.
Allow it to guide you and reconnect you
to the Spirit of All.

Earth Mother

Infinite joy around you abounds.
Dancing in circles, it flows from the ground.

The Mother of All speaks to you, too.
Open your heart; you'll know what to do.

As we listen with delight to the truth she imparts,
we gather courage slowly, to make a fresh start.

Growing together, we're stronger as One.
Each moment, give thanks, for what you've become.

EVERLASTING JOY

Everlasting Joy

Everlasting joy is the peace of an open, loving heart. Have you not heard the whisper of it all your life? Are you listening? Do you wish for more than a fleeting glimpse? What, then, is your path in this moment? Where is your joy?

Follow your thoughts and your heart to your joy. What have you placed or pushed aside in the name of duty? What parts of yourself have you forgotten or disowned?

Claim them. Claim your power, your birthright — the gifts of your soul you were born with. Your longings are part of you — they guide and motivate you on your path. Do not discard or dismiss them. Honor all the parts of yourself and "pull yourself together." You must love all the parts of yourself to open your heart completely. And then — you **will** find — everlasting joy.

Be Childlike

As children, you walk the path of enlightenment effortlessly. Your play is your work. Your joy is the flow you embrace in each moment. This is your natural state of being.

Grace is not something that needs to be sought or gained. Intuition and guidance steer and shape your world effortlessly. The natural flow of the universe carries and shapes you.

Look into the eyes of a young child and see the sparkle and dance they are. They do not need to search for it – they are the dance, they are the joy. As you watch closely, you often can see adults interacting with children in ways that pull them away from this. As children are taught to fear their spontaneity and to doubt themselves, they begin learning how not to rely upon and trust their innate wisdom.

Looking at yourselves now as children whose innocence and joy had been stifled will help you to see where your work is. Your "work" is to stop allowing others to shape you, mold you, direct you, judge you, and punish you without your heart's consent.

Regain your true selves, your freedom, your innocence, your joy and delight. Become childlike. See through the eyes of a child. Play and love, dance and skip, embrace and believe with the purity and clarity of a child.

Many believe you must become an adult to know the truth and see clearly. The opposite is true. The clarity that shines forth in the sparkle of a child's eyes is the beauty of unencumbered Spirit. Unencumbered is what you want to become now.

Seek ways to release your excess baggage. Let go of turmoil, pain, fear, doubts, worrying, and denial. Walk through your troubles and days knowing you and your life are healed, free, and born anew of your own choosing.

All of your substance, in all its forms, is held and sustained naturally in joy. Be playful and recapture the true essence of childhood — whether it is the joyful dance you remember or the dream of what you missed as a child — embrace it now, love yourself unconditionally and fully. It is not irresponsible to become the joy-filled child you were born to be. The responsible, adult thing to do, ideally, is become the pure and childlike Spirit you are.

Please, Please Me...

Pleasing yourself —
what a great way to start!
Pleasing yourself, yes, will open your heart.

Open to play, to the music, the song...
open to what you have dreamed all along.

Open to passion and loving and Grace.
Open to the Beloved in everyone's face.

Open to guidance, the answers, the Truth.
Open to what flows right to you is proof;

that you are worth pleasing, and pleasing again,
that you are worth loving as your own best friend.

Ignore what I tell you, you'll be in a stew.
Ignore what I say and you'll find yourself blue.

But, choose just to listen and open to you...
see what your guidance would first have you do.

I'll bet you'll be funny — even awkward at first,
as the answers flood in and you feel you might burst.

But, hold on to your hat, you are running this show,
make your own choice, set your pace and let go.

There's so much inside of you waiting to flow.
Open to your own love and watch yourself grow.

Please yourself daily with purpose and passion.
Please yourself daily with food and with fashion.

Love yourself wholly with what you say and you do.
Remember the words, *"To thine own self, BE true."*

Follow your heart with verve and conviction.
Give up all ideas of infirmity and affliction.

Follow your love in the light of the sun,
Find yourself there, in the heart of the One.

THOUGHT CONTROL
AND EMOTION

Thought Control and Emotion

Self-control – the control of all your experience – begins with thought. You must first perceive to conceive. The reality of every individual is formed, shaped, and changed by their past, present, and subsequent thoughts.

As you learn to clearly and cleanly choose your focus, observing as you go, you will become aware of an ease and gentleness in your process, as you sift through the debris of your past and no longer choose pain, drama, fear, judgment, and self-doubt.

Thought is the beginning of every hope and every dream ever manifest. When you choose to "back" a thought, you support it with e-motion – and whatever the emotion, it is energy now put into motion. So, think about and notice which thoughts and emotions are fueling and motivating your actions – anger, fear, and lack, or love, trust, and joy? As you identify what you are driven by, what fuel you are choosing? Be aware that if it is anything other than unconditional love, it will cost you energetically – and physically, if you focus on it enough.

The price you will pay is the prolonging of what you were trying to avoid, for those around you will only reflect what you send out.

The true challenge of the Spirit is to **know** yourself as love – to see it reflected in All around you and know that it is YOUR reflection you are experiencing. The love of all you see and experience is the love of the One – You!

Loving yourself is the greatest gift you can give. Watch the universe respond!

Affirmation

This or something better
now manifests for me,
easily and effortlessly,
in love and light, Grace and gentility,
in totally satisfying ways,
for the good of all concerned.
I offer my relationships and all of my life,
my trust and faith, peace, gratitude,
confidence, and patience.
We are One and united in love.

Set Yourself Free...

There is peace in rendering the truth of the heart.
There is Grace in surrendering to make a fresh start.
Joy everlasting can be your best friend
when you dance the divine around the next bend.

Embrace the true Spirit that wants to consume you.
Embrace the deep well of your soul and then soon you
will find you've become what you've searched so long for.
You've left pain behind and you've walked through the door.
You're now on the threshold of a grand mystery —
evolving and shifting effortlessly.

Pick up the pieces that you left behind,
that will nurture your soul and comfort your mind.
Let go of the rest, give thanks and be through.
You've had enough pain; it's no longer for you.
Escape from the chatter playing inside your head,
relax in the flow and reside there instead.

Don't forget who you are as you stumble and fall.
Use your own inner compass to scale the next wall.
These obstacles serve to remind you again,
to keep choosing your vision through thick and through thin.
Among all the stars, there's a vision you hold,
intentions of might in a tapestry of old.
The dreams of your heart, your divine mission,
spark the passion that fuels your intention and vision.

Precious One, seek to relieve your own inner grief.
Find solace in the love of the memories you keep.
For that love is the seed that will blossom and grow,
shower you with gifts and upon you bestow,
the Grace and abundance to make a fresh start,
the peace and the joy of a strong and healed heart.

You are the process by which love arrives.
You are the story of success that derives
great pleasure and purpose in all that you do,
seeking to know what is pure and is true.

You can stake claim to what is rightfully yours.
You can drop fear and doubt and be totally sure
the love that you seek is right where you are,
supporting you and guiding like a beacon or star.

Choose your next step with gusto and Grace.
Wherever you land, you are in sacred space.
Think not of where you've been,
but, where you'd like to be.
Let go of the past,
and set yourself free!

LIFT YOUR SPIRIT

Lift Your Spirit

Pull yourself together. Push ahead.

It is so easy to give up and succumb to lower frequencies and the denser vibrations of your mind as you relate to addictive perceptions of pain and discomfort held by many.

If you will honor your own individual Spirit in these moments by affirming that all is in divine order — especially at the times you feel your lowest — you will quickly raise your vibration and "Spirit!"

...LIFT YOUR SPIRIT!! ☺

Don't buy into the gloom and despair others may project. You may love and support them by first honoring your Self — and keeping your vibration up — in a place where they need to raise theirs to relate to you! Show them by your example that they are choosing where to be — but that your choice has been made — and that you can hold steady in a place of love and joy and de-light!

Shine on!

The Window of Love

There's a window to see through — a view from above,
that allows you to witness it all with great love.

It's the joy of divine, uncensored truth.
It's the picnic of angels as they feast their eyes upon you.
It's the magic of Spirit in It's greatest dance,
the unfolding of essence as we take every chance.

There's so much to look forward to, seeing from this view.
It's the window of opportunity in everything we do.
It's the majesty and magic that transforms the mundane.
It's the Grace that empowers the meek on this plane.

We can lift our perspective to see from this place,
There are no cheap seats; we are all offered Grace.
Check out this dimension, a bird's eye view,
look for yourself and see if it's true...

that you can unravel the mysteries of life,
you can let go of the pain and the strife,
you can embrace what is rightfully yours,
you can make life a heavenly tour.

All you need do is let go of your anchor,
release all your fears, look to Heaven and thank Her!
Feel yourself lift off, don't hold yourself down.
The air is much sweeter — no longer bound.

You've lifted your Spirit to the window in the skies,
that allows you to see through each Earthly disguise.
Join all the angels, their vantage point is true.
Honor and celebrate all that you do.

For love is the message and love is the gift.
See All through this window, give your life a lift!

PATIENCE

Patience

The purpose of patience is learning to let go of expectation and fear and to keep you in the present moment — in the flow.

When stressing yourself or others to meet a future vision, you are not living in the moment. When doubting or fearful, you are holding on to the past. Trusting in the flow, and the natural unfolding that occurs, brings about the state of patience and peace that unfolds through divine timing.

Juxtaposition — the spacing of time and place — creates the illusion that everything must fit into a certain order; but as this is an Earth-bound concept, patience serves to assist you in this process. As you practice trusting Spirit and yourself, and act upon the guidance of higher consciousness, you learn to relax and to feel safe and free. You *become* patient.

True patience is more than the act of tolerating a condition or an endurance of time. It is a state of *Be-ing*. If you are tolerating or enduring, you are in expectation or fear and not "in" the present moment. Being truly patient means you are at peace, living and trusting in the flow and the Grace of the moment.

Learning to Live in the Moment

Not living "in" the moment creates toxic thoughts. Toxic thoughts create dis-ease. Dis-ease is your body's signal to you to choose — to let go of pain, and let go of what is not essential for the present moment.

There are so many times each day when you are "presented" with opportunities to embrace the now. Often times we are focusing on what has already taken place or what we project for our future — for later that day, week, month, or year. Even "looking forward" to something keeps us from "being here now."

The "present" **is** the gift. It is all we have and what we can choose to be most grateful for.

Each moment we are here to love. To love ourselves as God, to love each other as God, to love all that is around us as God, for we are all One.

If you ask, "How can I feel loving in every moment?" the answer is, "By choice!" By choosing love in each moment, your heart opens. As you live from your heart, you resonate with the song of all life, the joy of all being, and in each moment, endless and infinite possibilities are available to you.

And, in this knowing and loving, an open heart is joyous and filled — not only with love, but also with gratitude. Gratitude is a grateful attitude. Through the strength of appreciation and affirmation, the open heart takes this a step further to a Grace-filled, grateful attitude of gratitude.

Living in the past or the future — holding your thoughts and attention there — is living from lack. Lack's core belief is one of not trusting that you are truly worthy, deserving, and able to experience love and its joys. In truth, you are the love you seek.

As God, as One, we all have the same choices, the same opportunities, the same propensity to love. No matter what your experience is, you can choose in every moment to hold your thoughts in the present — in gratitude, with a full heart. You have the gift of the moment; you have the gift to re-create yourself and your life in every moment of every day.

What will you do with this gift? Will you focus on what used to be? What could have been? What might be and what has yet to come? Will you judge yourself? Others? Or, will you choose something different?

Ask your heart, "What is the most gentle, loving, joyous, honoring, and nurturing thing I can do for myself in this moment?" Listen to your heart and follow it. Honor it as your most profound guide.

As you learn to embrace the guidance of your own heart and to embrace each moment in gratitude — as it is "presented" to you — you will find the flow of life is a current. You can choose to fight or go with the flow. As you surrender to the moment from this loving and ready place, you become the flow, the stream, the moment.

You are be-coming.
Be...come.
Be.

In Gratitude...

As I take time to thank the stars above,
I am grateful for all the blessings bestowed upon us —
for the gifts we truly love:

the gifts of peace, of hope and Grace,
the gifts of home — a safe, warm place,
the gifts of health and wealth galore,
the gifts of family, friends, and more,

the gifts of purpose and direction,
the gifts of an open heart's affection,
the gifts of joy and dance and song,
the gifts of feeling we belong,

the gifts of inner strength and might,
the gifts of passion and delight,
the gifts of rain and Earth and sun,
the gifts of knowing we are One,

and, the precious gift of the present —
to be right here and now,
to be able to choose to begin anew,
when we're not always sure how —
with a love so great, it sees us through,
wherever we go, whatever we do.

I am grateful for these blessings,
and for so much more it's true.
And as I count my blessings,
please know I'm counting you!

Wishing you the joy and peace of a full heart —
now and always.

BREATHING

Breathing

Relaxing always starts with the breath. Breathing is a two-part process. As you inhale, joyous strands of light and universal matter enter your physical body, nourishing and lifting you to a higher vibration. As you exhale, the "cosmic debris" you have accumulated in your physical structure is released through your breath. As it is released, it is immediately restructured and recycled into an unattached and available form of universal energy.

This is why it is so important to be clear in your thoughts and intent. Every thought forms, shapes, and "colors" the value you place on your sense of your unlimited Self. Your ego has a habit of limiting this awareness of Self by reducing its value down to the belief that you are a small self. Depending on which direction your thoughts are heading, each breath magnifies the creation of your value accordingly. This in turn shapes and forms your physical vehicle, your state of mind, the "climate" of your life and all your endeavors, relationships, and collectively, the climate of the world, the Earth, and mass consciousness.

So you see, with every breath comes the responsibility for the universe. As you receive the gift of life from Spirit on every inhale, while the force of All is in your lungs and filling your personal temple with love and life, you have the choice to return it to the All, the universe, the path in front of you, with the love, Grace, and gentleness in which it was so freely given. It is your choice, your will, that determines the scenery and climate of your journey, and it also affects the journey of all others. It is your every exhale that determines whether gentle breezes blow — or ferocious storms.

Become and remain conscious and aware of every breath. Fill your lungs and your life with the glory of infinite love.

Breathe deeply.

As I Breathe

Never again will I speak with contempt...
let me sow love with my words.

Never again will I hurt with untruths...
let me heal as I breathe.

Never again will I choose wounded ways...
let my heart open in joy.

Never again to judge or be judged...
let me accept the divinity in all.

Never again to cry out in fear,
never again to restrain hopes and dreams,
never again to limit or bruise,
never again to feel separate or alone.

Let love surround me.
Let peacefulness fill me.
Let joy dance through me.
Let beauty radiate from me.
Let the love of One motivate me
to enfold myself in Union with All.

THE UNION OF HEARTS, SOULS,
AND MINDS
IS THE GIFT OF MUSIC

The Union of Hearts, Souls, and Minds Is the Gift of Music

Have you ever danced in the magical flow of the love created through interaction with music — expanding as light mingles with sound, creating energy patterns, vibrations, and healing for the entire universe?

The song of All life fills all with harmony and peace — a union of spirits — the song and dance of the One.

In this place of union, the divine manifests into form. Through music, creativity takes shape, constantly changing, enveloping, merging, and uniting all life, all hearts, and all minds — to beat and breathe and resonate with the love of Source.

Hear the music in your own voice — in the wind — in all life. Let it move you to dance — the dance of life — of all creation. Feel it inspire you to create, to shape and mold yourselves into greater visions and expanding manifestations of love.

Feel the gift of Spirit as it sings to you in new ways. Look to yourself to discover new ways of bringing music and the joy of its dance to yourself and others.

Let all your senses be opened and flooded with the music of the One — the song of all life.

Overtones

Open to the music playing inside your head.
Open to the dance as you lie in your bed.

Give up illusions that limit your pace,
embrace, instead, no-time, and no-space.

Choose to let go of reluctance and doubt,
it is time to find out what your life is about.

Do you dare take the chance
that will bring you your dreams?
Will you harvest the toil of long-ago planted seeds?

Spread your wings and take flight, for your future is nigh,
no need to wait for the next by and by.

Grasp onto the hopes that hide inside your heart.
They're the guideposts of your journey, and as you embark,

feel the music of your soul strike up the band,
feel the universe respond to the wave of your hand.

The glory and magic you've dreamed of is yours;
it's the fountain of youth, it's those opening doors!

It's the ride you came in for, the dance of your life!
It's the song you choose to sing every day, every night.

Dare to bring all your passion to the song of your heart.
Fuel the fires of your soul as you make a fresh start.

You're not hanging in limbo, you are choosing each step.
Notice what it is you allow, what it is you "forget."

Dance the dance with great purpose;
let the rhythm take you there.
Feel the music stir inside you as joyful sounds fill the air.

You are standing on the edge of the precipice of love,
and as you leap, you will know, you're supported from above.

Listen to the music that's been there all along,
Don't sit this one out; they're playing your song!

Music

The song of all life,
encodings of the soul,
brings universal truth
into shape to unfold.

The music we make,
the vibrations we hear,
releases separation,
illuminates fear.

Flowing and dancing
creation divine –
the Union of hearts
and opening minds.

Glimpsing great beauty,
a gift to behold,
my heart expands
as it fills my soul.

The sound of the One –
Spirit in flight,
the music we are,
the song of all life.

JOINING TOGETHER AS ONE

Joining Together as One

For many, the union of hearts, souls, and minds has been experienced primarily on a physical level, but physical union is not necessary to take you into the heart of God – only an open mind, an open heart, and a Spirit that's free.

Seeing each other through the eyes of love takes you into the consciousness of all lovers – connecting strands of light to and through All – lifting and opening, raising the vibration of the planet, and healing all hearts.

The union of souls through the divine act of lovemaking is a sacred process that can open many levels of awareness. When two join together intentionally perceiving and choosing to be with, as, and in the presence of God, the polarities of the individuals, their soul purposes, and their unique perceptions of loving through the divine are balanced and integrated.

Returning to the One is the feeling lovers capture through this union. Consciously holding your lover through God's eyes immediately surrounds and lifts you to the place where this can be reflected and experienced. You have longed for this return all your life. Union, especially the union of hearts, dissolves fears, doubts, anger, feelings of separation, and resentment.

Learning to reconnect is the most important lesson for the planet now. You are not reconnecting to something you were ever separated from, but connecting to the knowing that you are, in and of yourself, this divine love at all times. Those who trigger this remembrance are beautiful reflections of your own light, your truth – your knowing.

Choose to own and reflect the beauty and Grace of the One — so that others may find themselves through the reflecting light in your eyes.

It is now time to allow for the reconnection to All and with All, the Union — the beautiful journey Home — through your own eyes — the eyes of love.

Oh Beloved

Oh beloved,
As you lie next to me,
I will hold you passionately with my arms.

I will hold your heart tenderly
and gently with open hands.

I will hold your gaze until the veil lifts
and I see your flame.

I will know your beauty
and find myself there.

INVITE TOMORROW IN

Invite Tomorrow In

As you drift into sleep each night, give thanks for the day you have experienced — releasing it lovingly and gently without judgment. Breathe through these moments of transition with clear intention — letting go in gratitude and gentleness. As you do this, you consciously choose to honor the gift of your life.

Invite tomorrow in with joy. Invite the dawn of the rest of your life. Invite the promise and hope, the laughter and the tears, the fullness of life. You need not know what the future holds — only that you embrace it.

Invite the peace, the love, and the comfort of gentleness. Invite the love of self and others that comes with an open heart. Invite your heart to open more fully with each morning. Invite your divine essence to shine forth without judgment or fear — in unconditional love. In your thoughts and heart, invite those in your life to join you in this process. And then, invite sleep.

Enter Into the Silence

Enter into the silence, young one,
for it is there you are held in perpetual bliss.

Enter into the silence, young one,
for it is in knowing your divinity
that you become awake.

Enter into the silence, young one,
for your peace is your haven,
and in running from yourself,
you have no home.

Enter into the silence, young one,
for you watch your dreams take shape
in this theater of love.

Enter into the silence, young one,
for you have nothing to fear
but your own fear.

Enter into the silence, young one,
for it is in choosing to really know yourself
that you will know true beauty.

Enter into the silence, young one,
for in going within,
you are reunited with All.

The Way Home

Joyous abundance fills the land,
with rays of hope for every man.

Loving light falls gently down,
sifts through Earth's maze and through our crowns.

Endless devotion surrounds us with care,
as we stumble and fall or open in prayer.

Limits we place on our hearts and our friends,
can be released in each moment and cast to the wind.

Doors open in front of us as we close others behind,
bringing dreams to fruition and great peace of mind.

Hearts can be broken and love still again,
revealing the strength of our Spirit within.

The gifts of each moment are infinite and thus,
deserve our intention to choose them with trust.

As we surrender our fears and embrace the unknown,
the path of our own heart will be our true Home.

Live Fully

Sense fully the divine every day —
all around you in every way.

See with your eyes
what you've been hoping to see.
Hear the world around you
perform its loving symphony.

Smell life's fire as it smolders,
before it bursts into a flame.
Smell the fullness of each moment
like a pregnant sky before the rain.

Feel the heart of every being
receive the gift of your love.
Know the joy of gratitude
for these gifts from above.

Let this emanate about you
and light up your face.
Let your radiance lift others
as they are touched by your Grace.

Open to the passion and the glory of life.
Release the need to control and the drama of strife.
Replace all your fears with persistence and trust.
Your choice to believe in each moment's a must.

Create joyful tomorrows as you live fully today.
Invite the child within you to come out and play.
Don't wait another minute to embrace life — you know how.
The best times of your life are for living — right now.

Visit Beloved on the Web:

Beloved's Music:
www.BelovedHeartsong.com

LaHo-Chi Institute of Energy Healing:
www.LaHoChi.org

Other Offerings:
www.OpenYourHearts.com

Email:
beloved@openyourhearts.com

About the Author

As the Director of the LaHo-Chi Institute of Energy Healing, Beloved Heartsong travels and teaches trainings throughout the country. Massage therapists, bodyworkers, and acupuncturists can receive nationally accredited Continuing Education Hours for the workshops.

Beloved also offers classes in Sacred Tantric Dance for Women and Sacred Journeys, Tours, and Retreats in Mount Shasta, California.

Beloved is a singer / songwriter / pianist / composer and has CDs of her uplifting and heart-opening music available through iTunes, CDBaby, Amazon, and on her music site: www.BelovedHeartsong.com.

Beloved's educational background is in Social Work, Psychology, Special Education, and Energy Healing, and she is the proud mother of three grown children.

Beloved's greatest joy is in sharing the dance of life with people by empowering them to re-member that the fullness they seek in life is within themselves, helping them recognize that the gift of love is in their own hearts and that they can choose to see and honor the reflection of love in everyone's eyes.

www.ingramcontent.com/pod-product-compliance
Lightning Source LLC
Chambersburg PA
CBHW061447040426
42450CB00007B/1255